LOVE

LUST

& other shades

HIS! HISSI

ANDRA RACOVITAN

This book has undergone three (3) total cover
changes since its initiation
in January of 2019.
Ultimately, Andra decided that a classic black and
white look would fit the theme best.
However, because she implemented a lot of
effort and time to her initial cover designs
she decided to keep the artistic aspect of that transition on here
as a reminder of the hard work and passion it took
to bring her first book all together.

And still can't look at the cover and think you know the book. — Andra

Hissing
or
Kissing

LOVE, LUST, & OTHER SHADES

ANDRA RACOVITAN

Library of Congress Control Number: 2018914192
ISBN: Hardcover   978-1-9845-6905-9
                 Softcover   978-1-9845-6904-2
                 eBook   978-1-9845-6903-5

To order additional copies of this book, contact:
Xlibris
1-888-795-4274
www.Xlibris.com
Orders@Xlibris.com
788673

Beloved reader,

Poetry is a lot like love. A universal language. And I think we all can agree that love can be a bit messy. At times hard to understand. It follows no rules and it has a rebellious streak. I know this first hand. Yet it is the one truly beautiful thing, even though nothing is guaranteed. It frees you from your own limitations. It challenges your thinking patterns and helps you embrace parts of your core that are substantial to living life with purpose. That's what makes it magical.

And so *love* is that one thing that everyone seeks after but few are brave enough to embrace. I dare you to embrace it. Because it's worth it.

I hope this book will help you understand that. Or at least make you smile on your rainiest days.

XO,

Andra

BUT TRUTH BE TOLD
LOVE
IS ALL I'VE EVER KNOWN
FOR YOU BABE.
KINDA LIKE THE OCEAN...

LOVE

{Shades of it}

i.   What 'falling' felt like

It was so easy to love him.

Like the ocean...

You know when you go to the ocean and feel its breeze hit
your lungs as you sit by the shore staring in awe at the mystery
and vastness of the water? As you watch the tiny diamond like crystals form
on its surface? That dance they do
to the never ending beat of the waves?
Something about that makes you never want to leave.
Perhaps that's why we fall in love with the ocean.
Because it's orphic—mysterious and entrancing beyond
ordinary understanding.
That's how I felt in his presence.
When we met, my heart whispered for the first time
"*he's the ocean.*"
She told me wild things before but nothing ever so drastic.
I never fully believed her stories anyway. I never really
met love anyway.
But with him, she told me and
for the first time I
actually...
believed her.

{that one kiss}

I remember when he walked in.
Those wild hazel eyes.
The first brush of my lips
Against his.
It was electric.
Time was of the essence.
If you were to snap a shot
To capture
That moment in time
You would understand
Exactly
What I mean.
That kiss
Time stood still.
Perhaps
I've been drunk since,
And I hate to admit
That
Out of all kisses
I remember
That one kiss.

What do you mean 'what do I mean'?!

It was a reaction.
A vibe.
That's all I remember.

But then he has these qualities,
so hard to miss.
He wears bravery like
a crown
and
honor seals his pretty mouth.
It's not that he's just something
as simple as
handsome.
He's so much more than that.
He's magnetic.
His field pulled me in differently like—

Like what?

Like— *at the core of me.*
And no one has that pull on me.

(*hah! Catch the expression on my face when I'm saying this? And take a
picture,
I wanna' know exactly what I look like when I talk this way.)

Anyways,
Am I making sense?!
'Cause...
That's what I mean.

give me that weekday lover

Some girls need the diamonds and pearls and the fanciest,
stupid stuff
to feel something.
And they want to call it love.
But dang,
I swear if you ask me
I'll tell you
something so complete, money wishes it had money to buy.
It's that weekday lover,
captured in one fragment in time so sweet,
even a snapshot might miss it.
It's that second *he* walks through that door,
a little tired, a little worn.
Ugh!
Gimme' that weekday lover!
I've learned that's what's priceless,
on a Wednesday at like—
5:48PM.

My heart?
She speaks things about me
I knew nothing about
Before you.

Awake.

Dreamer?
I'd say my dreams look like
shades of him
when I'm fully awake
almost falling asleep in his
castle arms.

ii.   Not really over, right?

Friends:

How is your beloved better than the rest?

She:

His lips are dripped in honey.
His smile lights up a kingdom.
His eyes mirror my soul.
His arms are like pillars of solid, solid gold.
His heart, when I hear it beating
Calms me like a child.
I swear he's Eiffel,
His touch looks better on me than pearls.
But now I can't find him anywhere.
Have you all seen him?

What do you mean
just forget it?
Is that what we should always do?
Give up?
That's the problem with
the problem.

Closing my bedroom blinds on the stars...

There are nights when the stars ask me why I close my blinds on them,
when they know how much I've always loved to wish upon them,
to stare up in wonder.
And the only answer that comes to mind is,
'now I know if I wish upon you nothing happens. And you shining your light on
the empty space next to me in my bed
reminds me of that.
But maybe one day, if I have him next to me again,
when I can kiss his back as I caress his skin,
while his eyelids are heavy as he's falling asleep
maybe then... I'll still marvel at your beauty.
But for now,
I like my room

jet black.'

#anothershade

Don't tell me that the sun doesn't rise in his
eyes like you've been there to see my glow
when he looked at me.
Or the way I'd fall for him
like the moon, every time.
Those nights,
we were not star struck lovers,
we were the eclipse.

Can we just start over
like
spring?
Because spring leaves winter behind, and everything
somehow blossoms again into something pretty.
And I really think
that's possible for people,
too.

But it's true,
the heart always looks back
to what it loves.
No matter the time,
stories, spaces,
or distance.
That's how you know.
Regardless of its mystery.

1 question

If I wrote a book telling the whole world
that I love you, will you believe me?

Dallas nights

All these girlfriends eyeing their boyfriends eyeing me. Yet
my eyes filter right through them hoping to catch *his* in every crowd
I see.

#*whereyouat*

{Girls— keep your boyfriends. I don't want 'em.}

A note on my IPhone

When I love it's *all or nothing.*
Like a coin I bet my life on and cross my fingers not to lose.
The middle ground is too rigid,
too safe, and
far too boring,
for

a flame like me.

{*I flipped that coin. It was worth it even if…*}

still

We were picture perfect.
The kind you want to forget
But there's *still*
These pictures on my iPhone and...
I can't forget to remember.
And I forget on purpose to... delete them.
We'd outshine them all
Like
Diamonds.
We'd steal every glance
There was to be stolen.
I remember –
We even made the sun jealous
That one day
In September.
Don't you remember?
But I think that wasn't the right kind of glow
To...
Keep us together.
Was it?

But there's *still*
These pictures on my iPhone and...
I can't forget to remember.

#theuglytruth

iii. *Messier Shades*

Love is my weakest argument.

I'm over you.
I love you.
I'm over you.
I love you.
I'm over you.
I love you.

This pendulum
Is getting out of hand.
It's not even a battle anymore.
It's insanity.
So if this acknowledgement is
The first step into
The acceptance stage
Does this mean I've finally accepted
The end?
Or have I just accepted
My insanity?

~~Voice of reason~~ *madness*

My heart insists that
We've let it go too soon.
My mind tries to shut my heart out.
I don't even know
Which one I should listen to anymore.
I have lost my voice of reason.
But maybe
I don't need a reason.

Maybe
I'm just meant to love you madly.

#lovebemadness

Ask me to make any promise
and I'll try my best
to keep it.
But don't ask me
to promise to stop loving you
because...
that's one promise
we both know
I can't keep.

Fazed.

The Universe and her
Playing tug of war
Wrestling arm to heart
What a forceful force.
But
Which one is stronger?
Who's keeping the score?

If our bridges burn,
I'll swim.

27

Some nights
I have no poems.
Some nights
I am sadder than sadness.

My heart insists that
I should bet it* all on this love.
And I actually want to listen to her.

Messier shades

I didn't know what to do with it.
So I turned it into art, like a mosaic of different shades.
Pin it on a wall as a reminder that even the messier things can become astonishing things.
Like you and I.
I still think we're awe worthy.

1 certain thing.

These days I'm not so sure about your whereabouts,
who you are with, where you're going, how things look in your world.
But one thing I'm sure of is that—
if I can't love you like I want to
I want heaven to do it for me, but
better.
That's the *1 certain thing*
I'll always want
regarding you,
in the midst of
life's ever changing
seasons.

Lust

That one summer night in June...

I craved him in ways different than lust. You know that feeling
that sits on top of your heart, ready to be spilled but too complicated for
words?
I went speechless the moment we locked eyes, again.
My eloquence— betrayed me, swallowed up like my pride.

But then
there was my touch.
And then there were my lips, ready to brush against every part of him.
And finally,
all the words that failed me ready to be pressed against his skin like
my poetry,
in that bed, between those sheets.
I wanted to seal us like a golden tattooed memory, without apology.

Because I understood this one thing now
better than before...
...tomorrow really
isn't promised.
Tomorrow,
we may lose it all,
again.

{*And sure enough, tomorrow came and... all was lost.*}

Royal hues

Something so royal
about the
hues of gold
hues of blue
hues of grey.
The intertwining
of our touch
in that moment
in that mood.
Something so divine
about the gentle brush
of my lips
against his.

He was grace on my lips and he tasted like heaven.

Don't look at me with those eyes.

I am disarmed.

Reign Wednesday- lost in dreams (wcw)

When he reaches for her
Does he know he's touching love?
Eyes dazed with lust
Wondering how it would feel
To feel so deep within
The mysteries of her.
She also wants the same
And hesitation slowly fades
And in a moment
He reigns over
Every inch
Of her silk glossed skin
Glowing from the heat of him.
His aura she can't resist
His strong arms
She loves to feel
As he
Grabs a hold of her.
Soft sighs from within
Let out from her lips
Onto his lips
While he whispers
Things *love* loves to hear.
And pouring
She reigns
Over him.

Love, Lust, & Other Shades

I only want your
Shades of gray
In the bedroom,
And in all the
Inappropriate places
Lust decides for us.

But in love,
Give me
Black &
White.

*I want
All or nothing.*

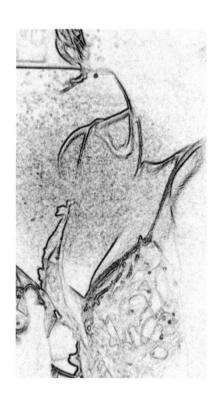

Oasis Dreaming

I had a dream
That
He was kissing my lips
That he was moving slowly
With
His fingertips
Past my hips.
The heat of his body
Against my skin
Was the kind of heat
That needed cooling
By an oasis
That poured
Just for him...
Just for him.

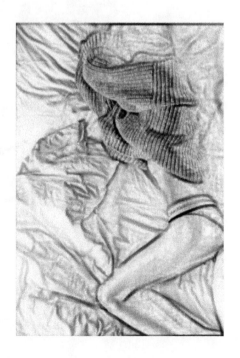

Hips & Skin

It was electric,
That touch of his in contact with my

hips & skin.

Other Shades 1

{When I went reckless}

The sun blinded me and...
that's all I remember.

How do you undo something after it is done?
I think the more you try to clean it
the messier it
becomes.

#whatsdoneisdone

Intrigue

I'm like a weapon in his hands.
I am not so sure he understands.
Or maybe he does.
Maybe he loves things just a little
dangerous and unpredictable,

a little bit
like me.

'A' Team

Popping bubblegum
In the front seat of his car,
He's got one hand on the wheel
The other on my heart.

He's driving us to where?
In this little town
In the middle of
Nowhere.

It could be anywhere
To be honest
And I don't even care.
He's a bit reckless.
Like me.

Still
I'll wear him
Like a pearl necklace
Around my neck
At a Gatsby
And I'll sip on his lips after the party
At like—6AM
Like I sip on my champagne
Only half awake.

He tastes better
Than that
Smooth tasting Rosé
Anyway.

Plus
He looks like Gatsby
With all the lights on.
But I don't know if he loves me
Like Gatsby loves
Daisy.

But it's whatever.
I told you
He's just a bit reckless.

45

And I'm reckless too.

Until we're wrecked.

Maybe I'm crazy,
Maybe he's magic.
You gotta' understand,
I'm cool with both.

Love's
the poison
and the poetry.
And...
she's always been intrigued
by
paradoxes.

#mymuse

{the magic in the bittersweet}

If love doesn't drive you a lil'
Craaaaazy
My darling,
He isn't it.

{tattoo this on my rib cage}

Bite me

Bite me
like a bullet
or just
bite my lip instead?
Shoot me like a weekend
whiskey on ice,
'cause I might get you dizzy that way.
Or spare me like
change
if you really want to.
Whichever route you take
please be mindful,
babe.
'Cause I can be so reckless
and
sometimes I...
I just can't help it.
I'm sorry.
Bite me or just...
Forgive me for it?

Oceans Deep

I dive into my impulses
Like they are a body
Of cool ocean water
In the middle of July.
I am
Completely engulfed
And yet I'd rather drown
In pure freedom
Than be eaten up alive
By contemplation,
Hesitation,
Frustration, or
All the other words that scream
B*tch-
Don't settle out of fear.

POKER FACE

He can keep it
Nonchalant
Yet he
Read me from the start.
What a shame.
He's the first one.
I swear
I was just as good as him,
Once.

But-
No bluff is safe to be held
So close to the heart.
Playing against the
King
Of my heart.
No bluff is safe
Here.
I fold.

That girl's not a real crowd pleaser

Some say she seems a mix of
Thorny rose
With a touch of
Sex & smoke.
Punk rock in her walk.
Her demeanor—
Wolf.

They say she's been seen
Kissing snakes
That hiss on her lips
But they think with snakes she
Best identifies.

But deep in her soul
At the core of her core
Only the privileged get to know
She's that solid gold-good
Of a girl.
Bad only when
She needs to be.
Loyal?
<u>Like nobody.</u>

She may *seem
A mix of things
Yet she's just a rose
With
Softened thorns
But never a real crowd pleaser.

{*a book and its cover*}

I say a lot of things
I don't always mean.
Who doesn't?
But
I love you
was never one of those things.
I always meant it
in all the little, big, messy,
reckless ways I've ever said it.
And I just pray
you know.

2AM

Do you drink because you miss him or
Do you miss him because
You're drunk?

#theordermatters

Drunk texting

sent

{*It's not the tequila, I wish it was...*}

Where*

    is

my

    mind?

  ?

    ?!!!

Madness is roses

There's a certain kind of beauty that
only madness
reveals.
Embrace it.

{noted— *when pushing my own buttons*}

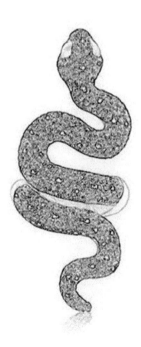

Loaded gun

My heart is a loaded gun
But the moment it fires
It turns into love.

How?

IDK.
These bullets
Are only firing at walls and
It leaves no room for harm.

I see...

But reckless are these lips
Always sealed by a crimson colored kiss.

Hm.

But these bullets
Firing out of me
Are heart shaped.

You know?

We all have that *one* chapter that
reads a bit off than the rest.
Right there in the middle.
But if you look close enough, it's
not off at all. It's so on point that
without it, an important bit of your life would be missing.
The growth.
The middle part of growth is always messy, and it looks like
anything but that.
Yet it is needed just as fire is needed to prove gold's worth.
Look at your reckless chapter and say,
I am gold.
Because you couldn't have been who you are today
without it.

OTHER SHADES II

{When I understood}

Like a tattoo

The big things are actually the little things in life,
like a tattoo that only becomes whole after so many tiny little pokes. It gets
messy, it bruises, but the end result is whatever you decide to create...
make it beautiful.

#hereandnow

Perfectly imperfect

Beloved reader,

One of the most valuable lessons to learn is that,
there is no perfect anything, anywhere.
No matter what!
Instead of setting the goal there,
find the *magic* within, in the real.
At the bottom of the chambers of your heart,
everything is a magical reality.

Perfection is illusory and it will forever leave you as it finds you—
a mess on a defeated journey.
Love— on the other hand, is raw, passionate, unapologetic, messy,
a *masterpiece.*
Never to be confused with something as boring as perfection.
It's masterpieces that leave the world in awe because of their hard to define,
perfectly imperfect
qualities.

Remember this the next time you start to wander.

A case for love — 1 valid argument

Someone once said that you should choose the one who
falls in love with you and knows *exactly* why.
But I disagree with that notion.
Because that's a condition placed upon love-
a concept hard to fully explain in concrete terms.
A concept that has been best conveyed by art,
and art is not
the easiest to interpret.
It just makes you feel more alive.
So to attach
(**place reason here**)
is to deny love's intrinsic quality,
its magic.
Sure, we can try and rationalize it but…
I believe we *love*
for no specific reason.

#nospecifics

Asking for closure is just another way of
saying,
'please...
let's not close this chapter.'

Love,

A rebel on the verge of
Sobriety and drunkenness,
Not knowing which to choose,
Yearning to be understood.
Trying to rearrange two halves
Into a perfect whole.
A heart undone?
So hot
So cold
But still beats in hues of gold.
How do you explain that?
Tell me.
No one really knows.
But I do know that
Nothing so greatly affects
Let alone inspires
So much passion out of
One single beating heart
If there is no
Love.

#allthefeels

Love - the accessory we don't choose

Everything's a growing process.
A work in progress.
There's always that

Before &
After.

And you look at yourself like
You'd look at
Two sides of the same coin—

So the same
Yet
So completely different.

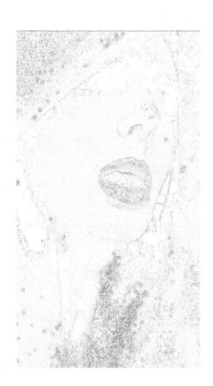

I am soft enough to
bend far enough,
without breaking.
And I've learned
that too,
is a strength.

Do you have any tattoos?

*She pointed to a poetry book and said,

*These words in this book have been inked on my heart,
Just like
a tattoo.*

Do we look for the wrong things
in the right people,
or vice versa?
Perspective is everything.

{ *food for thought.*}

Read yourself

Are you happy?

Everything we think and do
is interconnected.
It starts within,
and that energy is boldly
reflected
in the things that *manifest*.
So—
Speak life, walk in your truth,
and live so so
<u>fully.</u>

Power Measures

You know what makes you brave?

LOVE.   *LOVE.*

        #passion.

LOVE.   #soul

          .

        LOVE.

#faith

                        #thatonelover

.   *#LOVE.*

       #LOVE.

LOVE.   *#heart/mind*

                     LOVE.

        #love

Black & White

If this was a movie
It would be in classic colors.
A romance so
Black & white.

And *maybeee*
These are the kind of movies that ought to be created more often
After-all.

The boy and the girl don't always have to end up together to be happy.

Or do they?

Acceptance

Just accept *it*.
Whatever that looks like.

But I really hoped...

Truth be told
I can't deny
I really hoped...

'Cause
From the first night
We met
There was this
Sense of
Familiarity.
A click that
Flows so naturally,
Pretty enough for poetry.

Fire with fire.
Sun & moon.
The hearts beat a bit faster
Than they should.

I do but can't blame the Universe.
Yet at the end of the day,
When it is all said and done,
I hope it's understood
My heart always meant well...
And...
Yeah.

Other Shades III

{0 shades given}

So in life,
you are most alive in the moments where you
live right there on the edge,
where you can see everything so clearly
without tilting over.
And you've got to embrace anything that helps
you experience life that way.
In the center it's safe and all but
you don't see much.
You don't blossom where perspectives are limited.
But when you're on the edge it's like— the entire world is your platform, and
you're right there at the top of it, getting a glimpse of it all.
So if you have to do unorthodox things to make it clear that this thing, your
life
is *real*,
then by all means
do it.
You don't need approval on how to live your *gift*.
You have to do what reflects *you*,
in order to learn and grow *you*.
Life's too short for all that other *bs*.

{So...don't be afraid to shake the world a little, sweet darling,
with your beautiful voice,
your glowing presence,
and all these fine things that make this earth a little more
ravishing to walk on,
*** simply because you exist. ***
Create yourself unapologetically.
Leave your mark.
You owe it to...
yourself.}

You're not called to perfection.
You're called to progress.

{what a relief}

Let your stumbling blocks
Become building blocks
To something
More solid
For you and for those around you.
If not,
Then they are just something that
Happened to you.
And you're way better than that.
Way, way better.

Rule #1

Forget the rule.
In order to *get* real,
You must *be* real.
With yourself.
And sometimes no rules apply here.

Do something that scares you
Every day.
Sometimes
The things that scare you to pieces
Are the very things that you need
To evolve.
Everything looks different
When it loses power
Over your mind.
Fear is your biggest opponent.
Not people,
Not failure,
Not lack.
It's the fear of the results.

The irony is that
Fear is in fact,
A liar.
You can't fear a lie.
Always remember that.

Without taking risks
You actually risk everything.
That's the only risk
I don't encourage.

The thing is,
Everything in this world
Is so simple.
Sometimes that's a good thing.
Sometimes it's a disaster.

In life
there will be certain
things,
faces,
spaces,
experiences,
that not even time
will truly fully fade.
They are like a compass for your journey.

I have never seen a tamed spirit live an interesting life.
So…
No.
Thank you.

Wear your backbone
Like a crown.
It's *that* kind of a walk
That will get you places.

Overall,
Be *love*.
Do everything in love.
In the end
It's your greatest,
Most noble teacher.
That much I do know.

{1 Corinthians 13:2}

...and speaking of love, just for the record—
I still love him.
Kinda like...
the ocean.

{DMM}

CPSIA information can be obtained
at www.ICGtesting.com
Printed in the USA
BVHW081112240419
546394BV00005B/613/P

9 781984 569042